W9-CHZ-028

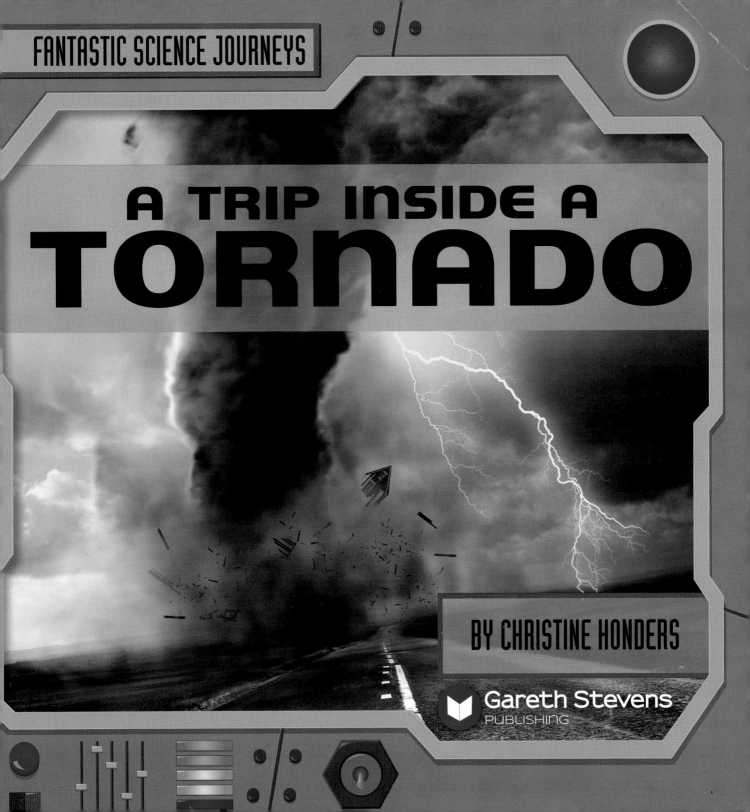

FANTASTIC SCIENCE JOURNEYS

A TRIP INSIDE A
TORNADO

BY CHRISTINE HONDERS

Gareth Stevens
PUBLISHING

Please visit our website, www.garethstevens.com. For a free color catalog of all our high-quality books, call toll free 1-800-542-2595 or fax 1-877-542-2596.

Library of Congress Cataloging-in-Publication Data

Honders, Christine.
A trip inside a tornado / by Christine Honders.
p. cm. — (Fantastic science journeys)
Includes index.
ISBN 978-1-4824-1998-6 (pbk.)
ISBN 978-1-4824-1997-9 (6-pack)
ISBN 978-1-4824-1999-3 (library binding)
1. Tornadoes — Juvenile literature. I. Honders, Christine. II. Title.
QC955.2 H65 2015
551.55—d23

First Edition

Published in 2015 by
Gareth Stevens Publishing
111 East 14th Street, Suite 349
New York, NY 10003

Copyright © 2015 Gareth Stevens Publishing

Designer: Sarah Liddell
Editor: Ryan Nagelhout

Photo credits: Cover, pp. 1, 5 solarseven/Shutterstock.com; p. 7 © iStockphoto.com/ QuantumWebmasters; p. 9 Dieter Spears/E+/Getty Images; p. 11 Rainer Lesniewski/Shutterstock.com; pp. 13, 19 Todd Shoemake/Shutterstock.com; p. 15 deepspacedave/Shutterstock.com; p. 17 (main) Minerva Studio/Shutterstock.com; p. 17 (vortex) Valentina Proskurina/Shutterstock.com; p. 21 EmiliaUngur/Shutterstock.com; p. 23 Cyclonebiskit/Wikimedia Commons; p. 25 jessicakirsh/ Shutterstock.com; p. 27 (main) Larry Miller/Photo Researchers/Getty Images; p. 27 (emergency kit) Julia Nichols/E+/Getty Images; p. 29 Fer Gregory/Shutterstock.com.

All rights reserved. No part of this book may be reproduced in any form without permission in writing from the publisher, except by a reviewer.

Printed in the United States of America

CPSIA compliance information: Batch #CW15GS: For further information contact Gareth Stevens, New York, New York at 1-800-542-2595.

CONTENTS

Let's Take a Trip! 4

Extreme Weather 6

What Is a Tornado? 8

Tornado Alley. 10

Before the Storm 12

A Supercell Thunderstorm 16

Mesocyclones 18

The Path of the Tornado 20

After the Storm. 22

Predicting a Tornado. 24

Be Prepared 26

That's an Extreme Trip! 28

Glossary. 30

For More Information. 31

Index 32

Words in the glossary appear in **bold** type the first time they are used in the text.

LET'S TAKE A TRIP!

You've probably seen many thunderstorms. A really bad storm can make a tornado. You may have seen pictures of tornadoes, but most people have never seen a real tornado.

What if you could get on a special ship and safely see what happens in a tornado? You'd see how a tornado forms and feel how fast it moves. This book will take you on that adventure. Let's take a trip inside a tornado!

THAT'S FANTASTIC!

The word "tornado" comes from the Spanish word *tronada*, which means "thunderstorm." English sailors changed it to "ternado" and used it when they talked about bad storms.

Our ship will keep us safe from the strong winds of the tornado.

5

EXTREME WEATHER

Weather is all around us, every day. It's something we can't control. In fact, it's so powerful that it often controls us. The weather affects what we do, where we live, and even what we wear.

Very bad weather is sometimes called extreme weather. Extreme weather—such as **hurricanes**, snowstorms, and tornadoes—doesn't happen very often, but when it does, it causes lots of harm to buildings and roads.

THAT'S FANTASTIC!

The worst tornado in US history happened in 1925 and was named the Tri-State Tornado. It traveled through three states—Missouri, Illinois, and Indiana—and left a path of ruin more than 219 miles (352 km) long!

Extreme weather often forces us to stay indoors.

WHAT IS A TORNADO?

Before going inside a tornado, we must know what one is so we can be ready. Tornadoes are nature's strongest storms. They usually come from powerful thunderstorms.

Tornadoes can have winds up to 300 miles (483 km) per hour. Tornadoes are so strong they can pick up cars and toss them through the air! This is one of the main reasons tornadoes are so dangerous.

THAT'S FANTASTIC!

Most tornadoes travel about 10 to 20 miles (16 to 32 km) per hour. Other tornadoes are so fast you would have to drive a car more than 70 miles (113 km) per hour to outrun them!

Tornadoes are very hard to outrun. It's best to find a safe place to hide from their dangerous winds.

9

TORNADO ALLEY

Let's fly our ship to where a tornado might start. The United States has about 1,000 tornadoes every year, more than in any other country. Most of them happen in what's called "Tornado Alley."

Tornado Alley is an area that stretches from Texas to South Dakota. One reason many tornadoes form here is because the land is very flat. Another reason is that warm air from the South and cold air from the North meet here, which is perfect for making tornadoes.

THAT'S FANTASTIC!

During what's called the "superoutbreak of 2011," more than 300 tornadoes formed in 21 US states from April 25 to April 28.

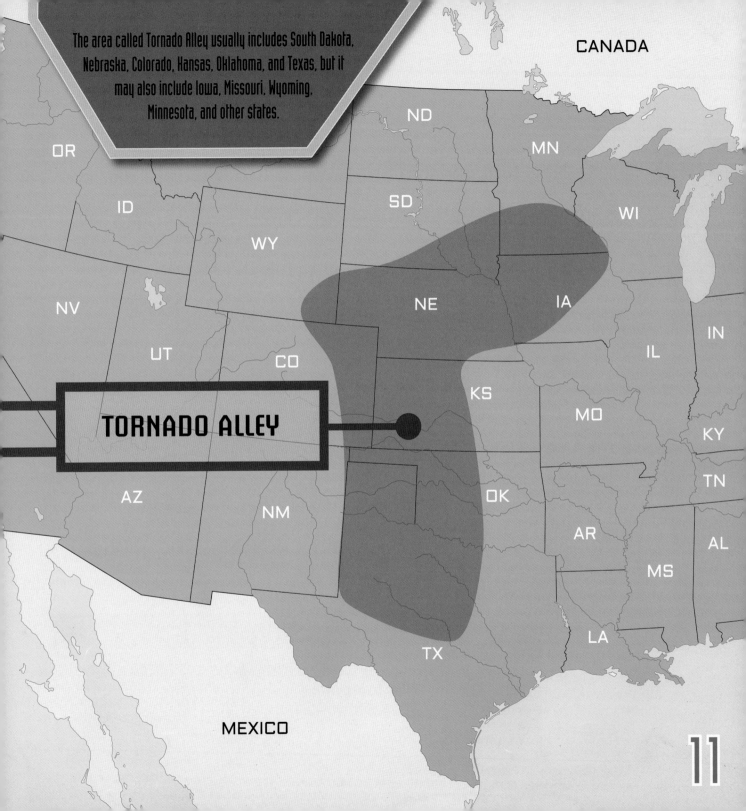

The area called Tornado Alley usually includes South Dakota, Nebraska, Colorado, Kansas, Oklahoma, and Texas, but it may also include Iowa, Missouri, Wyoming, Minnesota, and other states.

TORNADO ALLEY

CANADA

MEXICO

BEFORE THE STORM

Now that our ship has taken us to Tornado Alley, let's bring it close to the ground. The air is warm and **humid**. Now let's go back up into the air. The air there is colder and drier. This temperature difference is known as **instability**.

Suddenly, a warm breeze blows up from the ground and pushes our ship further into the sky! That's because the sun heated up the air near the ground, making it very light and causing it to rise quickly. This is called an **updraft**.

THAT'S FANTASTIC!

When it's heated, the warm air is less dense than the cooler air above it, which causes it to rise. "Dense" means how much mass is packed into a certain volume.

Instability in the temperature is often a sign that a storm is coming.

13

The updraft carries water vapor into the **atmosphere**. Water vapor can't be seen, but when it reaches cool air, it forms clouds and turns into rain. The rain starts to fall all around us.

As the rain falls, it pulls air down with it. The rain becomes so heavy that it creates a **downdraft**. The updraft and downdraft get stronger and carry the water vapor—and our ship—around and around in a circle!

THAT'S FANTASTIC!

Sometimes updrafts carry raindrops so high they freeze. They jump back and forth in the updraft and downdraft, getting bigger until they fall as hail. The largest hailstone ever measured weighed 2 pounds (0.9 kg)!

Updrafts and downdrafts moving quickly create dangerous opportunities for extreme weather such as tornadoes.

15

A SUPERCELL THUNDERSTORM

When we look out of our ship's window, we see that the updraft and downdraft are going up and down in a regular pattern. They begin to twist around each other and make each other stronger. We're in a supercell thunderstorm, the most dangerous kind of thunderstorm!

When we take our ship close to the ground, the wind is slower and blows in one direction. Now let's fly the ship higher. The wind speeds up and blows in the other direction! This is called **wind shear**.

THAT'S FANTASTIC!

Instability and wind shear cause a **vortex**. An example of a vortex is the spinning water that forms when you let the water drain out of your bathtub. As the water flows down the drain, it spins.

The vortex that forms out of a supercell storm is also called a **funnel cloud**.

vortex

MESOCYCLONES

We see a vortex start to form. In a thunderstorm, the vortex is called a **mesocyclone**. Mesocyclones are usually 2 to 6 miles (3 to 10 km) wide. Now that a mesocyclone has formed, there's about a 50 percent chance it will turn into a tornado.

The mesocyclone gets caught in an updraft and spins faster. It reaches out of the storm cloud in a swirling funnel cloud. Rain and hail pull the funnel cloud to the ground. Now it's a tornado!

THAT'S FANTASTIC!

We can't see the funnel cloud until it picks up dirt and dust from the ground. But we can hear it. A tornado's roar is like a freight train!

THE FUNNEL CLOUD

mesocyclone

rotation

cool, dry air

funnel cloud

updraft

warm, moist air

dust and dirt

There are lots of things happening inside a funnel cloud.

19

THE PATH OF THE TORNADO

The tornado follows the direction of the cloud that it came from, and so does our ship. In the United States, tornadoes move from west to east. Most tornadoes last 2 to 3 minutes, but some last much longer.

The spinning winds of a tornado are like a giant vacuum, sucking up objects, trees, animals, and sometimes even people! Usually it's dangerous to fly near the tornado winds, but our ship is made of special, strong metal, so we don't have to worry.

THAT'S FANTASTIC!

Tornadoes are usually only about 1.5 miles (2.4 km) wide. The edge of a tornado can destroy all the houses on one side of a street and leave the houses on the other side untouched.

The things picked up by a tornado's strong winds can be thrown very far away.

21

AFTER THE STORM

Scientists aren't exactly sure why tornadoes stop, but most think it's because the mesocyclone gets interrupted by something. It can be interrupted because it stops raining or because the air temperature changes.

After the storm, we fly our ship over the tornado's path. As we look through the ship's windows, we see some houses are completely smashed and other houses are completely untouched! We hope the people on the ground had enough warning so they could protect themselves.

THAT'S FANTASTIC!

The center of a tornado is called the "eye." Only two people have been in the eye of a tornado and lived through it. They say it's quiet, calm, and hard to breathe, with almost nonstop lightning.

The harm caused by a tornado can take a long time to clean up.

23

PREDICTING A TORNADO

Meteorologists try to figure out when and where tornadoes might form. When weather conditions may result in a tornado, meteorologists announce a "tornado watch." When a tornado has been spotted, a "tornado warning" is given.

The sky might be blue when a tornado watch is given, but don't be fooled! Tornadoes can strike with little warning. Before they form, the wind dies down and the air can become very still. You should watch the sky for a greenish color or low, dark clouds.

THAT'S FANTASTIC!

Most scientists use the **Enhanced Fujita Scale** to measure the strength of tornadoes. EF 0 tornadoes are the weakest and cause little harm. EF 5 tornadoes are the strongest and can blow entire houses away!

ENHANCED FUJITA TORNADO DAMAGE SCALE

SCALE	WIND ESTIMATE (MILES/KM PER HOUR)	TYPICAL DAMAGE
EF 0	Wind gusts 65–85 miles (104–137 km) per hour	Light damage. Some damage to chimneys; branches broken off trees; shallow-rooted trees pushed over; sign boards damaged.
EF 1	Wind gusts 86–110 miles (138–177 km) per hour	Moderate damage. Peels surface off roofs; mobile homes pushed off foundations or overturned; moving autos blown off roads.
EF 2	Wind gusts 111–135 miles (178–217 km) per hour	Considerable damage. Roofs torn off frame houses; mobile homes destroyed; boxcars overturned; large trees snapped or uprooted; light-object missiles generated; cars lifted off ground.
EF 3	Wind gusts 136–165 miles (218–266 km) per hour	Severe damage. Roofs and some walls torn off well-constructed houses; trains overturned; most trees in forest uprooted; heavy cars lifted off the ground and thrown.
EF 4	Wind gusts 166–200 miles (267–322 km) per hour	Devastating damage. Well-constructed houses leveled; structures with weak foundations blown away some distance; cars thrown and large missiles generated.
EF 5	Wind gusts 201+ miles (323+ km) per hour	Incredible damage. Strong frame houses leveled off foundations and swept away; automobile-sized missiles fly through the air in excess of more than 328 feet (100 m); trees debarked.

The Enhanced Fujita Tornado Damage Scale was established in 2007 and is based on the original Fujita Scale created in 1971. It measures tornadoes based on the harm they cause and estimated wind gust speed.

BE PREPARED

Now that the storm is over, let's land our ship so we can help. Why are people coming out of their basements? That's because the first rule of tornado safety is to go to the lowest part of your house. If you don't have a basement, go to a windowless inside room such as a closet.

If you're outside when a tornado hits, you should lie down in a ditch. Always protect your head. If you're in a car or a mobile home, leave and find the nearest sturdy building.

THAT'S FANTASTIC!

People in Tornado Alley have emergency plans and safety kits ready if a tornado hits. If you're caught in a tornado, text, don't call. Keep the phone lines open for emergency workers.

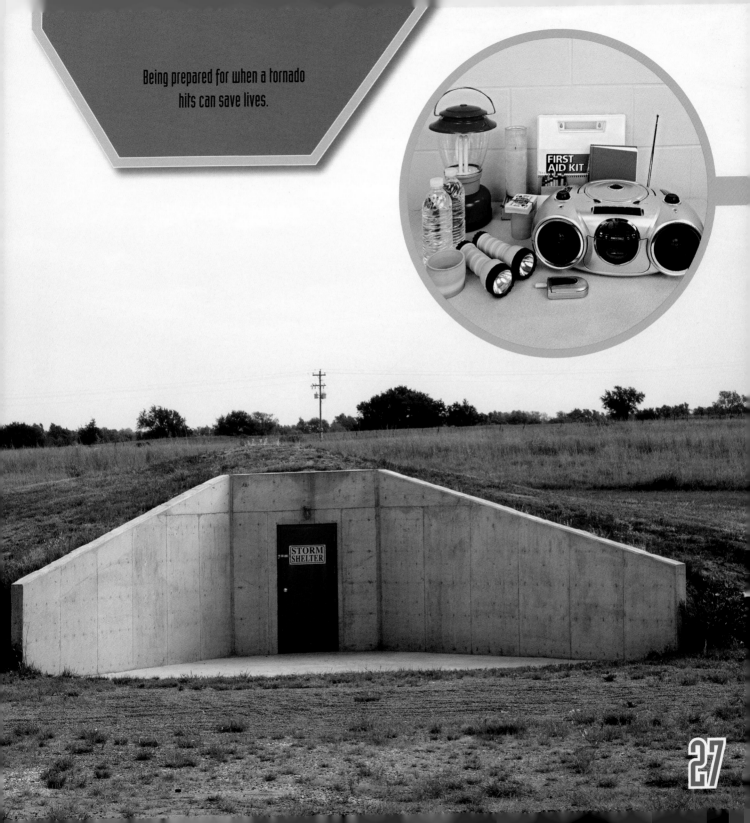

Being prepared for when a tornado
hits can save lives.

THAT'S AN EXTREME TRIP!

What an adventure! Our ship started in a thunderstorm and ended in a tornado. The whole trip only took a few minutes! Isn't it amazing that such extreme weather can happen so quickly?

Even though very few thunderstorms turn into tornadoes, they can happen anytime and anywhere. Next time, you won't have our sturdy ship to protect you. So if you see a funnel cloud, remember our trip inside a tornado. You'll know what to expect and how to keep yourself safe.

THAT'S FANTASTIC!

In 1931, a tornado in Minnesota lifted a railroad train with 117 people on it. It carried the train for 80 feet (24 m)!

Tornadoes are amazing—but very dangerous—natural wonders.

GLOSSARY

atmosphere: the mixture of gases that surrounds a planet

downdraft: the downward movement of air

Enhanced Fujita Scale: a scale used to measure the strength of a tornado

funnel cloud: a cloud with a long shape that is wide at the top and skinny on the bottom, like an ice cream cone

humid: having a lot of moisture in the air

hurricane: a powerful storm that forms over water and causes heavy rainfall and high winds

instability: a sudden change in the weather

mesocyclone: the whirling winds inside a thunderstorm that often produce tornadoes

meteorologist: a scientist who studies the atmosphere and weather

updraft: the upward movement of air

vortex: a spinning mass of water or air

wind shear: a quick change in wind speed and direction

FOR MORE INFORMATION

BOOKS

Armentrout, David, and Patricia Armentrout. *Tornadoes.* Vero Beach, FL: Rourke Publishing, 2007

Armour, Cy. *Tornadoes and Hurricanes!* Huntington Beach, CA: Teacher Created Materials, 2012.

Gibbons, Gail. *Tornadoes!* New York, NY: Holiday House, 2009.

WEBSITES

Make a Tornado in a Bottle
sciencekids.co.nz/experiments/makeatornado.html
Learn how to make your own tornado, and learn more about vortexes.

Storm Tales
www.history.noaa.gov/stormtales.html
Learn more about some of the worst storms in history on this site.

Watch Out... Tornadoes Ahead!
nws.noaa.gov/om/brochures/owlie-tornado.pdf
Make sure you know what to do if a tornado comes to your neighborhood.

Publisher's note to educators and parents: Our editors have carefully reviewed these websites to ensure that they are suitable for students. Many websites change frequently, however, and we cannot guarantee that a site's future contents will continue to meet our high standards of quality and educational value. Be advised that students should be closely supervised whenever they access the Internet.

INDEX

clouds 14, 18, 20, 24

downdraft 14, 15, 16

Enhanced Fujita Scale 24, 25

extreme weather 6, 7, 15

eye 22

funnel cloud 17, 18, 19, 28

hail 14, 18

instability 12, 13, 16

mesocyclone 18, 22

rain 14, 18, 22

safety 26

supercell thunderstorm 16, 17

superoutbreak of 2011 10

thunderstorm 4, 8, 16, 18, 28

Tornado Alley 10, 11, 12, 26

tornado warning 24

tornado watch 24

Tri-State Tornado 6

updraft 12, 14, 15, 16, 18

vortex 16, 17, 18

water vapor 14

winds 5, 8, 9, 16, 20, 21, 24, 25

wind shear 16